Claim your FREE bonus match!

SCAN ME

There have been so many great World Cup games in the past nine decades.

One of those is included in this free bonus! Can you guess which game it is?

Download now to find out!

If the QR code doesn't work use this URL

https://qrco.de/bdL9Md

Contents Page

Introduction

The FIFA World Cup is arguably the greatest sporting event in history. No other competition has grown as much over the years and served up a seemingly endless number of classic moments, images and battles. From Uruguay shocking the Brazilians in their own backyard in 1950 to Zinedine Zidane planting his head into Marco Materazzi's chest in 2006, the World Cup always guarantees many fantastic memories when it rolls around every four years.

Some matches in this book are here because of the number of goals scored, while others made it due to the rivalries or unforgettable incidents attached. All of them will never be forgotten, though.

So many games throughout the history of the World Cup have been classics, and there are a hundred others that mean everything to the individuals who watched them. Of course, not all of them can make it into this book, and because it is impossible to separate each of them, they have simply been put in chronological order.

Football is unique to each and every person who follows it for a variety of reasons. Some of us adore the clashes of old foes coming together for yet another battle, while others love nothing more than a goal fest where both teams throw caution to the wind. For many, it is simply the glamour of the World Cup and the beautiful melting pot that is 32 nations from around the globe coming together in one place to compete.

Who can see the image of Pelé being lofted into the air by his teammates and not be yearning for another World Cup to begin? How can someone not wonder how football's reputation survived after the bloody Battle of Santiago when police had to intervene on four separate occasions?

There are some moments in this book that you might not have heard about because they happened in an era long gone, and there will be many you remember vividly. They will all bring you joy and nostalgia simply because the World Cup will forever create memories that every other sport can only dream of achieving.

URUGUAY v BRAZIL

16th of July 1950
Final Group Stage Match
Maracanã Stadium, Rio de Janeiro, Brazil
Attendance: 173,850

The rivalry between Brazil and Uruguay stemmed from a lot more than football. With nothing but a thin border separating the countries, tensions had run high for centuries before the Jules Rimet Trophy went up for grabs for the first time in 1930. In fact, it was Uruguay's victory in that maiden final and their subsequent crowning as the original champions of world football that grated on the Brazilians the most.

As hard as it might be to grasp today before Brazil finally lifted the trophy in 1958, they were seen as massive underachievers, an issue in their mindset that the Brazilian novelist Nelson Rodrigues referred to as a "mongrel complex." The fact that Uruguay had already won a World Cup with a population of only 3.5 million compared to Brazil's 220 million was something that always stuck in the latter's throat too.

The World Cup in Brazil in 1950 was unique in many ways, but mostly in the way the format was designed. Unlike all of the tournaments before and after, this one was decided in a final group stage. It was confusing and messy, which is probably why it was never done again, but it still produced one of the most famous finals—technically not really a final, just the last group game—of all time.

In the lead up to the tournament in Brazil, the hosts were being touted as heavy favourites. They lived up to this billing by thumping Sweden and Spain 7-1 and 6-1, respectively, in the final group stage. Their opponents in the last match, Uruguay, had only drawn 2-2 with Spain and barely scraped by against the Swedes, claiming a tight 3-2 win.

All of this meant that the last group game wasn't a final in the traditional sense, with Brazil needing only to secure a draw while Uruguay needed to win. The other two teams' previous results had been too bad, and their game against each other became obsolete.

Football in Brazil was as fanatical then as it is now, and the pressure on the team was immense. In fact, several national newspapers had already printed the following day's editions, with pictures of the team on the front with the headline WORLD CHAMPIONS above it. Victory songs were composed and practised, and even politicians gave speeches about how proud they were of their world champions in the build-up to the match.

The game itself is known as the de facto final in that it created a near global fascination with all things World Cup. Football had been big before the 1950 finals, but it was about to explode in unimaginable ways. Still, television coverage was almost non-existent, and the world had to listen to the games unfold on through radios rather than watch them on TV.

The match at the Maracanã Stadium in Rio de Janeiro is known as the highest attendance for any football match in history. Officially, the numbers are recorded at 173,850, but with no seating back then and hundreds of thousands of people outside the ground trying to force their way in, it is widely agreed that well over 200,000 watched the action unfold.

Uruguay's coach, Juan Lopez, had told his team in the dressing room before kick off that they needed to lock up against their opponents. Brazil had mopped the floor with every team they'd faced, and he was insistent that they try to nullify the endless attacking options they would be faced with. The players agreed, but captain Obdulio Varela took center stage after the gaffer had left.

Legend has it that he produced several copies of a leading Brazilian newspaper with the headline "These Are the World Champions" pasted over a photo of the Brazilian team. After tossing the papers on the floor, he encouraged his teammates to spit and urinate on them before contradicting his coach and explaining that, yes, they needed to soak up some of the Brazilian pressure, but only for a period of time.

Using tactics that would have made Muhammad Ali proud, the Uruguayans spent the first half letting their opponents punch themselves out. They played backs-to-wall football, crowding their own box and reducing the Brazilians to long-range efforts and hopeful crosses.

It seemed to have backfired two minutes into the second half, though. Brazilian striker Friaça netted with a low shot that slipped under the Uruguay keeper's arm, and the packed Maracanã erupted into a frenzied celebration. But Varela wasn't done with the mind games, and he held the game up for several minutes as he argued with the ref, claiming that Friaça had been offside. He even went so far as to demand that the referee listen to what he had to say by way of an interpreter. His pleas were denied, but the huge gap in time he'd created between the goal and Uruguay kicking off again had nullified the crowd. Varela is then said to have taken the ball, planted it in the centre circle, turned to his teammates, and shouted, "Now it's time to win!"

Brazil's only frailty was their defence, and Uruguay took full advantage of it. Alberto Schiaffino scored in the 68th minute, further silencing the Brazilian crowd. Then, with only 11 minutes remaining, Alcides Ghiggia slotted the ball under the flapping Brazilian keeper's arm to make it 2-1. The deathly quiet around the Maracanã has become the stuff of legend, and the massive underdogs held out to shock everyone and claim their second World Cup.

After the match, two men were found hanging in the stadium. Several other suicides were reported around Brazil, and the crazy obsessiveness towards football that we associate with it today was truly born.

As the events unfolded, a 9-year-old Pelé walked into his living room to find his father crying. The radio in the corner informed his kid that Brazil had somehow lost the final. Shaken at seeing tears in his father's eyes for the first time, little Pelé told him not to worry and that he would win a World Cup for him one day. He won his father three of them.

HUNGARY v URUGUAY

30th of June 1954

Semi-final

Stade Olympique de la Pontaise, Lausanne, Switzerland

Attendance: 45,000

The 1954 World Cup is regarded by many as the greatest ever, maybe not in size or even the skills on show, but it brought about a lot of significant firsts. It was the first time the matches had been shown live on TV and had the most goals per game of any World Cup to date, with the Golden Team, Hungary, netting a whopping 27 of them. Even with teams playing more matches in the tournament these days, I don't think anyone will ever come close to Hungary's astounding record.

Hungary had already thrashed everyone in the group stages thanks to star performances from Sándor Kocsis and Ferenc Puskás, with thumping in an incredible 17 goals in 2 games. When they came up against two-time champions and holders Uruguay, another cracker was played out in front of 45,000 people. In a tournament that had already given the spectators an endless supply of goals, these two heavyweights doled out six more in what is often called one of the greatest matches ever played.

Ferenc Puskás had picked up a fractured ankle two games before, and although he wanted to play against the Uruguayans, he had to sit it out on the bench instead. Hungary were hoping to make the final, and if they did, they wanted their best player somewhat fit for it.

The only problem was that their semifinal opponents were seen as the real final, as either Austria or West Germany awaited the winners, and they were seen as pretty weak opposition. Whoever won the semi between Hungary and Uruguay would surely be the eventual champions.

Even without their talisman, Hungary still had a breath-taking frontline, with tournament top scorer Sándor Kocsis and Zoltán Czibor leading the line. The latter got the Hungarians off the mark with a flick on from the former, and Czibor took the ball down and drilled it into the bottom corner. It looked like the Hungarian steam train would show no signs of stopping, and the team who had slammed in nine goals in their opening group match looked nailed on for the tournament.

Uruguay, in the first half of the century, were one of the most organised teams around, though, and their emphasis on defence rather than attack was seen as almost blasphemous. Still, it had won them two World Cups up until that point, so they weren't going to change their style anytime soon. Where most teams would have crumbled under the endless waves of Hungarian attacks, Uruguay held firm until the halftime whistle.

Their resilience broke in the first minute of the second half when attacking midfielder Hidegkuti ghosted in at the back post to score a superb diving header and give his team a 2-0 lead. Hungary trotted back to the halfway line feeling like the job was done and probably thought that Uruguay would roll over and die like every other team had done during their two-year unbeaten streak. They were wrong, and the Uruguayans came back at them—hard.

In the 75th minute, Uruguay forward Juan Hohberg coolly slotted home from 12 yards, giving his side some real hope and rattling the Hungarians. Uruguay had created a few chances since Hungary's second, but they were also leaving gaps at the back as they pushed more men forward. They had no other choice, though, and their newfound adventurous approach paid off again in the 86th minute.

After a frantic end-to-end 10 minutes, in which both teams cleared the ball off their own line, Hohberg struck again. Collecting the ball from an intricate pass, he showed terrific composure to round the 'keeper and clip the ball into the top corner. Even though Uruguay were the current world champions, the equaliser was still a massive shock, but Hungary regrouped, and the game went into extra time.

The efforts it had taken Uruguay to pull the game back from the brink had taken its toll, and in extra time, Hungary regained the initiative. Goal machine Sándor Kocsis, who had surprisingly not scored in the semi yet, set things right in the 111th minute, heading the ball into the net from five yards. It was a kick in the teeth for the gutsy Uruguayans and one they wouldn't recover from this time.

Five minutes after regaining Hungary's lead, Kocsis scored again, effectively ending Uruguay's hopes of doing what Italy had done before them and winning the World Cup twice in a row. His second goal was almost a carbon copy of his first, as Kocsis snuck in at the back post to head his side into a 4-2 lead.

Uruguay had no answers, and the Hungarians played out the rest of the game with a little more caution than they had previously. They would need all of that resilience in their upcoming final against West Germany, but it seemed that Hungary were starting to buy into their own legend a little bit. It would be their downfall in the long run.

The Golden Team would never get another chance to win the World cup as they did in 1954, and the same could be said for Uruguay. The world of football was changing, and superpowers such as Germany, Brazil, Argentina and France would dominate the second half of the century in terms of World Cup trophy hauls.

Along with Holland, the Hungary team of the 40s is seen as the best side never to have won the World Cup, and only the Dutch have played in more finals and ended up on the losing side.

The game between Hungary and Uruguay was an all-time classic, and Hungary can always lay claim to being the first side in history to play what we now recognise as "real football."

WEST GERMANY v HUNGARY

4th of July 1954
Final
Wankdorf Stadium, Bern, Switzerland
Attendance: 62,500

It would be unthinkable today, but when the World Cup began in Bern, Switzerland, in the summer of '54, the pre-tournament favourites were the Hungarians, and not just by a little bit either. They were nailed on, and only for some typical German resilience, they would have taken home the Jules Rimet Trophy to place alongside the Olympic gold they had won the previous year.

West Germany were only getting back into competitive football following the war, and they had missed out on the 1950 World Cup due to the heavy restrictions imposed upon them in the aftermath. Compared to the Hungarians, who had some of football's first- ever bona fide world stars on their team, the majority of the German side was made up of semi-professionals.

Hungary lined up with Ferenc Puskás, Sándor Kocsis and Nándor Hidegkuti in a three-pronged attack. They also employed a roaming position strategy that had never been seen before, meaning players could switch roles during play if they felt the urge to do so. With two marauding full-backs—another first—they had been rightly labelled the "Golden Team."

Apart from winning gold at the Olympics and claiming the Central European International Cup—a sort of pre-Euros—in 1953, they also took the English apart in their own backyard that year. In a match that would shake English football to its very foundations, the Puskás-inspired Hungarians produced what is generally considered the first-ever 90 minutes of Total Football. It was like nothing that had ever been seen before, and the 6–3 win was also the first time England had lost at home to a team outside the British Isles.

Proving it was no fluke, the Hungarians offered the England team a chance for retribution in Budapest during the build-up to the '54 World Cup. They won that one 7–1, then hopped on a plane to Bern to bring home the big one—the Jules Rimet.

Hungary shredded their opponents, winning 8–3 in a game that epitomised everything about the way they played. Puskás was immense, dropping deep at times and switching positions, as well as netting a goal himself.

The German defenders were clueless, and the only blot on Hungary's copybook was the hairline fracture to star player Puskás's ankle. The injury would keep him out of the quarter and semifinals against Brazil and Uruguay, respectively.

Thankfully, they still had Kocsis, who had banged in four in the demolition job of the Germans at St. Jakob-Park. Germany recovered in their group playoff match against Turkey, another team they would meet twice at the same World Cup. They grew in confidence after that, beating Yugoslavia 2-0 before thrashing Austria 6-1 in the semifinal.

The final took place in the comically named Wankdorf Stadium in front of 62,500 fans. All of them expected a Hungarian win, and in truth, it was probably that same belief that caught Hungary out in the end. They were massively superior to their opponents, and the 8-3 thrashing the week before coupled with their name all-but-engraved on the trophy proved to be a very definite mental stumbling block.

The game itself started as everyone presumed it would play out. Puskás gave his team the lead with a smart finish on six minutes. Two minutes later, the Hungarians added a second, Zoltán Czibor taking advantage of some shambolic German defending before clipping the ball home. The Germans trudged back to the halfway line looking defeated, and with less than ten minutes gone and the firm favourites already two goals to the good, they must have feared another drubbing.

It didn't play out that way, though. Only a few minutes after the restart, Max Morlock slammed the ball into the net to give the Germans hope. Usually, when opponents did that to the Golden Team during that era, all it did was enrage the beast, but Germany flooded forward again fearlessly. They got their reward in the 18th minute when Helmut Rahn rose highest to nod in a deep corner that eluded the Hungarian keeper.

After a hectic opening 20 minutes, the game settled down a little.

Germany locked up and tried to compose themselves. The quickfire attacks they'd just unleashed weren't their style, and they knew the Hungarians would steamroll them if they continued to open up. Hungary tried to play through the white wall of German shirts, but their opponents had suddenly found a way to shut them off.

The second half mainly produced the same scenario—Hungary probing while the Germans locked up. German goalkeeper Toni Turek was inspired, denying Puskás several times with world-class saves. The German defenders flung themselves in front of everything, and with each passing minute, the Hungary team became more and more frustrated.

On 84 minutes, yet another Hungarian attack was broken down by the resolute German defence. The ball was played forward to Helmut Rahn, who feinted to go one way—wrong-footing a couple of Hungarian defenders—and drilled the ball past Gyula Grosics. The 62,500 people in the stadium watched in shock as the underdogs wheeled away in celebration. Puskás had a goal disallowed for offside two minutes later, and Toni Turek had time for one last wonder save right before the final whistle.

Hungary had lost their first competitive match in 31 games—quite literally at the worst time imaginable. As for their opponents, the world had just seen the type of performance that would become synonymous with German football throughout the following decades. It was also the first of Germany's World Cup trophies and the second final Hungary had lost following the disappointment of 1938.

West Germany wouldn't win it again for 20 years, as football was about to enter the era of a Pelé-inspired Brazil. That meant three of the following four World Cups would belong to the South American giants, and everyone else—including the Golden Team—just had to sit back and watch.

CHILE v ITALY

2nd of June 1962
Group Stage
Estadio Nacional, Santiago, Chile
Attendance: 66,057

In a tournament that highlighted just how brutal football had become, one game in particular shone a light on the nastiness teams had started to exude in order to get a result. Of course, football really would soon become the beautiful game we know today, and it was still wonderful back then, but it sometimes spilt over into a dirtier, more violent sport.

Chile were a handy side and playing at home—something that had proved highly fruitful for host nations in the past—but Italy were wily, and they had been there and done it all before. Tensions were already high before the game had even kicked off when Italian journalists Antonio Ghirelli and Corrado Pizzinelli wrote that Santiago was nothing but a dump where "phones don't work, taxis are as rare as faithful husbands, a cable to Europe costs an arm and a leg and a letter takes five days to turn up" (Crist, 2018).

Not very kind words, and a definite spark that lit the fuse on one of football's most shameful moments in time.

The lead up to the game became a pathetic punching match between both nations' media outlets. Chilean journalists hit back, calling the Italians fascists, mafiosos, oversexed and drug addicts. Italy claimed their displeasure stemming from the fact that Chile had been awarded the World Cup in the first place, given the terrible facilities. Following the 1960 Valdivia earthquake—the most devastating earthquake ever recorded—what stadiums the Chileans did have were in severe disrepair by '62.

Whatever the reasoning for such bad blood, it was all in extremely bad taste, and the match ended up being no better.

The first nasty tackle occurred after only 12 seconds, and it was a taste of what was to come. Back in an era when there were no yellow cards and a player had to basically assault someone to see red, it is even more amazing that Italian Giorgio Ferrini managed to get sent off after only eight minutes of play. He fervently argued his case as Chilean star Honorino Landa writhed in pain on the deck, but the English referee Ken Aston held firm.

Ferrini refused to leave the pitch and had to be dragged off by several policemen before the game could resume. Ken Aston tried his best to get a hold on the game, but it continued to spiral out of control. The next incident was even worse than what Ferrini had done, but it went unpunished. The ref either didn't see the punch being thrown, or he didn't want to send another player off so soon, but when Chilean forward Leonel Sanchéz slammed his fist into the jaw of Mario David, the game continued uninterrupted.

Aston later claimed that he had, in fact, not seen it. Back before Video Assistant Referees (VAR), if the ref and his linesmen didn't witness something, there were no repercussions. It was rumoured that one of his assistants had seen what happened but was too intimidated to report it. Whatever happened, the horrendous behaviour of both sides was just getting started.

A few minutes later, the same two players clashed, and as Sanchéz lay on the ground following a hard tackle, Mario David kicked him in the head. This time Aston had to react, and he sent the Italian off to more angry gesticulations from his teammates. These caused more scuffles to break out all over the pitch, and the sly Sanchéz managed to get away with another punch, this time breaking Humberto Maschio's nose. It was pandemonium, and the teams hadn't even gone in for halftime yet.

The game had to be stopped three more times as it progressed, with scuffles, punches and spitting throughout. The police were forced to come onto the field each time to separate the players, and it seemed that everyone involved forgot that there was an actual ball on the pitch.

The World Cup in Chile was marred by such nastiness the whole way through, but the game that would be dubbed the "Battle of Santiago" was undoubtedly the worst of the lot. In the first eight games of the tournament, spectators saw several red cards, a fractured ankle, cracked ribs and three broken legs. Many teams left it with their reputations marred, including Argentina, Yugoslavia and, of course, the two teams featured here.

With only nine men for the whole second half, Italy still tried to do everything they could to repel the Chileans. Their resolve was broken in the 73rd minute when Jaime Ramírez nodded in the opening goal. There were mass celebrations on the pitch and in the stands, and for just a moment, the horrors that had preceded the goal disappeared. But the damage had been done, and even when Chile added a second soon after through Jorge Toro, the footballing world had already been disgusted by what they had seen.

In the aftermath of the Battle of Santiago and the whole '62 World Cup in general, FIFA knew things needed to change. The man who refereed the match, Ken Aston, actually invented the yellow and red card system after witnessing the carnage between Chile and Italy. I suppose that we can look back and think that some good came out of such a despicable display from both teams, and we should never forget the unforgivable role the journalists played in the events that followed their nasty comments.

Chile qualified from the group in the end, finishing second behind West Germany. The Italians crashed out and returned home, still cursing the ref and the facilities. The hosts managed to get to the semis, where they came up against eventual champions Brazil. All in all, it was a brutal World Cup, but the repercussions and rule changes it forced FIFA to make were hugely positive for the development of football as a sport.

After showing the highlights of the match a couple of days later on the BBC, commentator David Coleman famously described it as "the most stupid, appalling, disgusting and disgraceful exhibition of football in the history of the game". It was a damning synopsis of the match, but for anyone who has seen the footage, it was also perfectly apt!

PORTUGAL v NORTH KOREA

23th of July 1966
Quarter-final
Goodison Park, Liverpool, England
Attendance: 51,780

People could have been forgiven for dismissing North Korea before the World Cup in England had even kicked off. In fact, the bookies had them at 1,000-1 outsiders to lift the Jules Rimet trophy. They were made up of part-time players with a sprinkling of semi-professionals, while their opponents, Portugal, boasted the great Eusébio in their ranks.

The World Cup in England had drawn unimaginable viewing figures, and the plan to transmit several of the matches via satellite had proved a masterstroke. Football was becoming beyond popular, and the fervent we associate with it today had well and truly taken hold. The '66 event would end in England's single greatest footballing achievement, but before that fateful game at Wembley against the West Germans, there had been plenty of other classic games and moments to savour.

One of the most astonishing came at Everton's Goodison Park.

Eusébio had already taken the World Cup by storm by the time the quarterfinal against surprise package North Korea kicked off. He had netted three of his country's nine goals in their opening three games of their group, with Portugal winning them all against some tough opponents, including Brazil and Hungary.

North Korea, for their part, had started as people had expected them to go on, losing 3-0 to the Soviet Union. Fearing the worst, the North Korean Football Association didn't bother to book accommodation for the knockout stage, as they had the talented Chile and two-time champions Italy left to play in their group. They drew 1-1 with Chile and shocked the Italians by beating them 1-0, essentially dumping the Azzurri out of the competition in the process.

Despite these two results, the build-up to the quarterfinal clash predicted nothing but a dominant Portugal win. The Koreans had fared well, but they were minnows at the end of the day. Eusébio was in the midst of being constantly placed on a pedestal next to the likes of George Best and Pelé, and the rest of his teammates weren't half-bad either—at least in attack. The game was seen as one of the pre-tournament favourites against a group of whipping boys who had gotten lucky.

In front of a packed Goodison, North Korea came out of the blocks flying. Pak Seung-zin crashed his long-range effort in off the underside of the bar in the first minute to stun the Portuguese players. With their opponents reeling, the Koreans continued to press and got their second on 22 minutes when Li Dong-woon bundled the ball home after some confusion in the Portuguese box.

Eusébio had tried almost on his own to pull Portugal back into the game after the first goal, but the second one was a kidney shot that completely floored his side. Three minutes after going 2-0 up, Korea netted again; this time Yang Seung-kook slotted home from eight yards to send the North Korean and neutral fans into raptures. The Portugal players hung their heads, and the biggest shock in World Cup history was on the cards.

Before the tournament, North Korea had spent two years in a secret, intense training camp in preparation. They stayed there the whole time away from their families and lived and breathed nothing but football. Every night after mealtimes, they were made to sit down and discuss tactics for two hours, and it was believed that a good showing at the World Cup would be the greatest honour and help dismiss the view at the time that Asian teams would never be able to eat at football's main table.

They fared well, but some teams are just better than others. All of the relentless coaching and training camps in the world cannot teach the things players like Eusébio possess, and when said player is on his game, there isn't much the opposition can do about it in the end.

The Portuguese legend took the game by the scruff of the neck, and after pulling one back two minutes after North Korea's third, he slammed in a penalty just before halftime to cut the deficit to one. As the players left the field for the halftime break, it actually felt like Portugal were the happier of the two sides, even though they were 3-2 down. They knew they were the superior team and that getting their second goal right before the break would have crushed Korean spirits.

It had, and 11 minutes after the restart, Eusébio completed his hat trick and levelled the scores with a tidy finish from a tight angle. He added a fourth three minutes later. After a marauding run that started in his own half, the Portuguese genius skipped by several Korean players and would have scored one of the competition's most incredible goals if he hadn't been scythed down in the box just as he was about to finish. He dusted himself off and slammed the penalty home to give Portugal the lead for the first time in the match.

José Augusto added a fourth in the 80th minute, heading home a corner to end the North Korean dream. The underdogs had performed wonderfully well to get to where they did, and the first 27 minutes of the match were breath-taking from the team the bookies had presumed wouldn't even score a goal in the competition.

For Portugal, it showed their immense attacking attributes but also highlighted how weak they were defensively. Eusébio would score again in the semis, but unfortunately for him and his team, his goal was sandwiched between two Bobby Charlton efforts. Portugal won the third-place playoff against the Soviet Union, but it was scant consolation for a team who had been one of the picks before the tournament began.

Eusébio won the Golden Boot following his nine-goal haul, and he would go on to be remembered as one of the greatest players of all time. But football will always find a team's frailties in the end, and it is nearly impossible to be successful without a solid backline. Portugal discovered that the hard way, although if we look at their teams since then, it could be said that maybe they never really took it on board.

ENGLAND v WEST GERMANY
30 July 1966
Final
Wembley Stadium, London, England
Attendance: 96,924

The rivalry between England and Germany went far beyond football by the time they met in the 1966 final. World War II was still fresh in the memory of the English, and the thousands of casualties and ruined cities of the Blitz were never going to be wiped away by a captain's handshake and an exchange of wreaths.

The bad blood spilt over onto the pitch, but thankfully only in a gentlemanly way. It was played in good spirits despite the clear hatred between the sides, and what remained when the final whistle blew was probably the most memorable match in the history of the World Cup.

England were hosting the World Cup for the first and last time to date, and they were determined to make the most of it. Before the 1962 event in Sweden four years previously, the English had made a habit of dismissing the competition as much as possible. Having travelled to a few tournaments and fared poorly, their need to wave a hand at the standard of football played by the rest of the world was starting to look a little like fear.

Brazil, Uruguay, Hungary and even the Germans had evolved their games as the century progressed. England, believing themselves to be the hub of football, struggled to understand why. After the mercurial Sir Alf Ramsey took charge in 1963, all of that changed. He kept the cornerstones of the English game that still worked but sprinkled it with foreign influences, such as pass and move and using tighter wingers.

For their part, the Germans had caught on quicker, and they had already lifted the Jules Rimet Trophy once already in '54. They played a mix of smooth, attacking football with a touch of pure aggression, but they hadn't come up against a defensive unit like the English yet. In fact, Sir Alf's side hadn't conceded a goal until the semifinals against the Eusébio-inspired Portugal side.

One of the main talking points in the lead up to the game was the injury to Jimmy Greaves in the group stage. The newspapers continued to print stories pertaining to his imminent return in the days before the final, with his replacement, Geoff Hurst, probably the only English person alive at the time who didn't want him to recover in time.

Greaves was England's primary frontman, and his goals-to-games ratio has never been equalled. Hurst had performed brilliantly in his absence, but Jimmy was the darling of English football, and the fans wanted him to play in the final. As it turned out, the loss of Greaves was hardly noticed in the end.

The game took place at Wembley Stadium in front of the second-largest crowd a World Cup final had ever seen. The 96,924 spectators looked small next to the recorded 173,859 (probably more) of the final in the Maracanã 16 years before, but it was still a massive number. Over 31 million Britons watched the game on TV (400 million worldwide), making it the largest-ever audience for a single event in British history.

The England side kicked off with an array of stars in their team, including captain Bobby Moore playing alongside Jack Charlton in defence and Jack's younger brother Bobby in midfield. The likes of Alan Ball, Martin Peters and Gordon Banks were also in the starting 11, making it one of the strongest England teams in history.

The Germans had players such as Franz Beckenbauer, Siegfried Held and Uwe Seeler, so they fancied their chances too. In a tense opening few minutes, both sides still managed to play open, expansive football. England felt like they could contain the Germans and hit them on the counter, while their opponents knew they had the craft to open them up if given enough time. It didn't take long, and the Germans took the lead on 12 minutes when Helmut Haller slotted the ball home to silence the English crowd.

Showing the type of composure he became so famed for, England captain Bobby Moore took a quick free kick six minutes later, drifting the ball into the box for Geoff Hurst to head it into the net. The game tightened up a bit after that short period of pandemonium, and the sides went in 1-1 at halftime.

The second half opened up a bit again, but it was still mostly cagey. That was until Alan Ball whipped a corner into the box that the Germans didn't deal with properly. The ball fell to Geoff Hurst eight yards out, and his shot deflected to Martin Peters, who stuck it in the net sending the crowd into raptures. But it wasn't over, and in typical German style, the away team showed nonstop resilience, scrambling the ball over the line in the 89th minute to send the match into extra time.

In a 19-minute period, two of football's most iconic and controversial moments happened on the turf of Wembley Stadium. Both of the incidents would involve Geoff Hurst, a man who wouldn't have been playing if Jimmy Greaves had been fit.

The first came in the 11th minute of extra time when he crashed a shot off the underside of the bar. It bounced down and back out again, and the England players wheeled away in celebration, having believed it to have crossed the line. The Soviet referee wasn't sure, so he consulted his linesman, Tofiq Bahramov, who confirmed that it had. England were 3-2 up.

The second moment that would forever remain etched in the memories of the footballing world was when Hurst broke free on the 119th minute as the Germans threw everyone forward. He carried the ball on his own, leaving the flailing opposition in his wake before slamming the ball into the roof of the net to complete his hat trick (still the only one in a World Cup final) and give England the trophy (also the only one).

In truth, there is only one way to finish off anything involving the '66 final, and that is with Kenneth Wolstenholme's immortal commentary for the final goal: "And here comes Hurst... some people are on the pitch; they think it's all over. It is now!" (Sir Geoff Hurst, n.d.).

BRAZIL v ENGLAND

7th of June 1970

Group Stage

Estadio Jalisco, Guadalajara, Mexico

Attendance: 66,843

Brazil and Pelé were looking to capture their third World Cup in four attempts in 1970. England, for their part, were trying to retain the title they had won four years earlier at Wembley, but this time without home advantage. Almost unbelievably, Pelé was playing in his fourth World Cup. What was even more outrageous was that he was still only 30, causing some of the more idiotic pundits to claim he was past it.

This was the first World Cup to be held in Mexico, and the soaring temperatures had been a real issue for the England players already. Their game against Brazil was only their second match of the tournament, but they had struggled with the heat in their opening match against Romania, only scraping a 1-0 win thanks to a Geoff Hurst goal.

In front of nearly 67,000 spectators in the Estadio Jalisco, the two teams who had shared the previous three World Cups between them locked horns. England started the game with six of the eleven players who had starred at Wembley against the Germans. Gordon Banks, Bobby Moore, Alan Ball, Bobby Charlton, Martin Peters, and Geoff Hurst had all lifted the trophy on that fateful day. Brazil were still the favourites, though, which wasn't surprising given the attacking talents they had to choose from, including legends such as Pelé, Rivellino and Jairzinho.

Despite the intense heat, England really took it to their opponents early on, and in the first 25 minutes, they were the better side. Bobby Charlton was pulling the strings despite clearly being baked alive, and he came close a few times with some thunderous long-range efforts. Brazil had their chances too, and Pelé was coming into the game more and more as the minutes ticked past.

No longer just a goal poacher, the Pelé that had been brutally kicked out of '66 had learned to manage his game better, and he was a more well-rounded player. Now, he had evolved into a classic Number 10, dropping deep into pockets of space and using his vision and composure to pull that saw him called into action almost constantly.

the strings. He was still a massive goal threat, of course, but his role in the team had naturally evolved.

After England's flurry of chances at the start, Brazil began to get a grip on the proceedings. Their marauding full-backs, Carlos Alberto and Everaldo, were proving to be a bit much for the English. In an era when defenders rarely crossed the halfway line, England found their own full-backs getting overwhelmed as they were repeatedly doubled up on. And it was during one of these moments when possibly the greatest save in World Cup history occurred.

Brazil's captain, Carlos Alberto, came swanning forward with the ball at his feet. As he slowed his pace and had a look around, the English players failed to pick up the electric Jairzinho as he overlapped down the right. Carlos Alberto found him, and Jairzinho skipped by Terry Cooper like he wasn't there. He looked to have overrun the ball before reaching it just in time and clipping it to the far post. Pelé rose highest and headed the ball downward, and with plenty of power. He was on the verge of wheeling away in celebration when Gordon Banks dived to his right-hand side and miraculously turned the ball over the bar.

England managed to keep Brazil at bay until halftime, but the heat was really starting to affect them. The players looked exhausted, and unfortunately for them, they were in for even more pressure in the second period.

After the restart, Brazil continued to stream forward. England knew that there was always the chance of a counterattack, and with it being only the second game in the group, a draw wouldn't have been the end of the world. Bobby Moore made several unbelievable tackles throughout the match, especially in the second half's backs-to-the-wall display Pelé would later embrace Moore after the final whistle, creating a picture-perfect moment in time that showed two geniuses appreciating each other and all they represented. England's reserves were broken on the 55th minute when Pelé's new creative role proved the deciding factor, much as it would in the final a couple of weeks later. After some trickery on the wing from Tostão, he spun the defenders a few times before finally clipping the ball into the box. It landed at the feet of Pelé, only 8 yards out. He could have shot, but there were several England players in front of him. Instead, he didn't panic and held the ball at his feet for a couple of seconds before casually playing a blind pass to his right that Jairzinho slammed into the roof of the net.

The single goal proved to be enough. England made an effort to get back into the game, but Brazil held firm. The packed stadium had been thoroughly entertained, but the tides of football since '66 had clearly shifted. It seemed that Brazil's poor performance in that World Cup in England had only been a hiccup, and they looked back on track to lift the trophy once more.

England, for their part, returned to winning ways in the final group game, beating Czechoslovakia 1-0. But the heat, an ageing side and the ever-evolving style of continental football proved too much for them in the end. They would only play one more match—the first knockout stage—where they would face their old rivals and opponents in the '66 final, West Germany. More on that next.

WEST GERMANY v ENGLAND

14th of June 1970

Quarter-final

Estadio Nou Camp, León, Mexico

Attendance: 23,357

Along with Brazil versus Argentina, England against Germany is probably seen as the fiercest rivalry in world football. A lot of that has to do with the war, but a big chunk of it can be attributed to the times and situations they always seem to meet each other. Whether it's the semifinal in World Cup 1990, the final in '66, or the penalty shoot-out to decide the game at Euro '96, the story of the English against the Germans can sometimes feel like fate has determined where and when they should clash.

These oldest of football foes would once again produce a World Cup classic that afternoon at the Estadio Nou Camp in León.

England had Geoff Hurst starting up front, and the Germans must have quivered at the sight of him, given what he had done to their side four years previously at Wembley. West Germany still felt aggrieved about how that final had played out, relentlessly claiming that England's third goal hadn't crossed the line. Both teams' animosity had never wavered, and the quarterfinal tie in Mexico was no different.

Germany had improved greatly from '66, and they now had the sensational Gerd Müller up front. The man known as Der Bomber was becoming known as the stereotypical goal poacher due to his ruthless finishing of any ball that happened to end up around the six-yard box. They also had the enigmatic Franz Beckenbauer in defence, who had who had single-handedly created the position of sweeper. He had played in the '66 final, but by 1970, he was a much more rounded and influential part of the German team.

There might have been only 23,357 people in the stands as the teams stepped onto the pitch, but that was almost double the attendance of any of the previous four matches that had been held there. The Estadio

Nou Camp isn't a big ground, so the number of people that had gotten in had filled it to the brim. Tensions were as hot as the weather, but the game played out in the most professional and elegant way imaginable.

England lined up in the red and white strip that had served them so well in the '66 final, but they'd had to replace Gordon Banks with Peter Bonetti that morning due to him having food poisoning. It didn't matter too much early on, as England took the game to their opponents with some relentless attacking and got their reward after half an hour.

Right-back Keith Newton carried the ball forward unchallenged before clipping a dangerous ball into the box. It was met by Alan Mullery, who slammed it into the top corner from six yards out. It was an excellent start for England, and they held onto their lead until halftime.

After some much-needed shade and fluids, both teams came out for the second half looking slightly more refreshed. The heat was relentless, though, and the players' tired legs and minds soon caused a few mistakes to creep in, but England's second goal was nothing but class and one that Germany could do nothing about.

It started with Geoff Hurst dropping deep and picking up the ball. Much like Pelé had done throughout that World Cup, he held the ball for a moment and waited for the galloping Keith Newton to overlap down the right. Hurst played him in, and the defender whipped the ball across the six-yard box to Martin Peters, who finished with aplomb. It was no more than England deserved, and up until that goal in the 49th minute, it was the best they had played in the tournament by a long way.

West Germany gradually started to get a grip on the game, and with 69 minutes played, wing-back Klaus Fichtel drilled the ball at the goal from

40 yards out. It was a hopeful effort, and it didn't make it further than a couple of feet. Unfortunately for England—and mostly Bobby Moore—the thing that stopped the ball was the England captain's groin. The ball squirmed loose to Franz Beckenbauer, and he shimmied before drilling it into the bottom corner.

England might have sensed what was coming, as Germany had long been making their name as a team that could grind out results from seemingly impossible situations. And that is exactly what they did.

It took 14 minutes of German pressure—broken by a Geoff Hurst header that skimmed the post—before the equaliser. A long, hopeful hoof into the English box was met by the five-foot-seven Uwe Seeler, who somehow managed to head the ball backwards. It looped over the helpless Bonetti, and the German captain wheeled away in celebration. Amazingly, the game between the two sides mirrored the '66 final, and it went into extra time with the score at 2-2.

Germany took control in extra time, with Beckenbauer pulling all the strings. He was majestic, and England couldn't cope with his deceptively casual wanderings. But it was Der Bomber who scored the winner after 108 minutes, nipping into the six-yard box to pounce on a loose ball and slam it into the net. England tried their best to get back into the game and created several good chances, but the Germans held firm. The English had hoped to retain the trophy on foreign soil, but the heat and the resilience of their old foes had proved a step too far.

ITALY v WEST GERMANY

17th of June 1970
Semi-final
Estadio Azteca, Mexico City, Mexico
Attendance: 102,444

Much like the England versus West Germany final four years before, a slight edge was added to this semifinal due to the events of World War II. Not as much, but there had always been some bitterness between the two nations in their previous meetings. Again, like the final in '66, both teams let their football do the talking, and the result was what would forever become known as the "Game of the Century."

Italy came into the semi having already won two World Cups ('34 and '38), while the Germans had taken home the trophy in 1954. In the first World Cup to be held in Mexico, the heat during the tournament caused exhaustion and injuries throughout. Thankfully, FIFA had recently brought in a two substitution rule, and unlike some of the World Cups before, teams could actually make a couple of changes if players took a knock.

Italy had topped their group earlier in the tournament but found it hard to score. Still, their famed defence stayed unbreached until the knockout stage, and even then, they only conceded one against the hosts, Mexico. Germany, on the other hand, had netted eight times in their three matches leading up to the semi, including a 3-2 extra time win against the English, which went a little way to healing the wounds suffered four years before at Wembley.

As the match played out, nobody could have guessed that the cagey affair would later be dubbed the "Game of the Century." After Italy had taken the lead in the eighth minute through Roberto Boninsegna's goal, it looked for all the world that the Italians would lock up and see the rest of the match out. And that is exactly what they tried to do.

Germany tried their best to breach the stingy Italian backline, but for any football fan who has seen Italy play, that is not easy to do.

The Azzurri are the original masters of defending, which is something that has never changed since the game of football first landed on their shores.

To make matters worse, Germany's best player and all-around legend Franz Beckenbauer dislocated his shoulder during the match. The Germans had already made their two allocated substitutions, so he was forced to pop it back into place, put it in a sling and play on. Hard to imagine now when we watch today's modern footballers flopping around on the ground if the sleeve of someone's jersey clips their ear.

In typical German fashion, they equalised in the 90th minute. In even more Germanesque style, the man who scored the goal, Karl-Heinz Schnellinger, had never scored for his country before. In fact, he never did again. With him playing his football in Italy at the time for AC Milan (222 games, no goals), it only added to the bizarreness of it all. It was a precursor to the madness about to unfold in extra time.

To this day, no World Cup game has ever produced as many goals in extra time. After what had come before, the Schnellinger goal and all the ridiculous comedic connotations that came with it seemed to loosen the bolts that had previously made the match so unbearable.

Gerd Müller struck first, making it 2-1 to the Germans on the 94th minute. Four minutes later, Tarcisio Burgnich equalised for the Italians before Gigi Riva scored a cracker with his left peg to put the Italians in front once more. The game had been flipped on its head, and for everyone watching, it suddenly felt like every attack—from either side—would result in a goal. It was end-to-end football in its purest form.

Italians in front once more. The game had been flipped on its head, and for everyone watching, it suddenly felt like every attack—from either side—would result in a goal. It was end-to-end football in its purest form.

The second half of extra time picked up where the first left off, and West German goal-scoring machine Gerd Müller netted again, making it 3-3 to tie up the game yet again. In the euphoria, Germany switched off, and straight from tip, the Italians streamed forward again.

In the heat of the Estadio Azteca, and with over 100,000 spectators in the stands and hundreds of millions more watching on their TV screens, Italian forward Roberto Boninsegna whipped in an inch-perfect cross which was met by Gianni Rivera, who slotted it home. It was so soon after the German goal that most channels were still showing the replay of Müller's goal.

The game ended 4-3 to the Italians, but the intense heat and the efforts needed to overcome the Germans proved too much come the final a few days later.

BRAZIL v ITALY

21st of June 1970
Final
Estadio Azteca, Mexico City, Mexico
Attendance: 107,412

When Brazil played Italy in the final of the 1970 World Cup, it was the first time two former champions had met at that stage in the competition. Not only that, but both sides had won it twice each and were looking to be the first nation to make it three. For Italy, it had been far too long a wait, having taken their trophies in '34 and '38. Brazil's success had been more recent, winning in '58 and '62, with the small matter of missing out in England in 1966 the blot on their copybook.

Mexico 1970 was a roaring success, so much so that they would host the tournament again 16 years later. After the brutality of '62 and the vast improvement of '66, the maiden Mexican World Cup saw more progress. Broader TV coverage, silky skills and, of course, Pelé's last World Cup all made for one of the greatest tournaments ever.

Italy came into the final having shocked West Germany in the Game of the Century in the semis, and the hectic nature of the extra time pandemonium that evening in Mexico City undoubtedly played a part in how things turned out in the final. Coming up against the Brazilian frontline of Pelé, Tostão, Rivellino and Jairzinho wouldn't have helped matters, either.

As we covered in the Brazil vs England section, Pelé had adapted his game by the 1970 World Cup to more of a Number 10 role, and it would never be more evident that day in the Azteca. In front of 107,422 fans and millions watching around the globe, the world's best player pulled the strings like a conductor in the New York Philharmonic.

The final kicked off at 12:00, so the sunshine drenched the pitch as the players settled into the game. The heat didn't seem to bother the Brazilian full-backs, Carlos Alberto and Everaldo, who continued as they had done throughout the World Cup, marauding up and down the touchlines and overloading the Italian defence.

Despite his more creative role, it was Pelé who got the first goal of the game, heading home Rivellino's cross in the 10th minute—Brazil's 100th goal in their World Cup history. As he wheeled away in celebration and jumped into the arms of Jairzinho, one of the World Cup's most iconic images was captured as he punched the air with delight. Brazil had the lead, yet there was no chance of them resting on their laurels.

They continued to dominate the game, yet they rarely looked rushed, casually popping the ball around the pitch with intricate five-yard passes. Italy tried to win it back, but it seemed that every time they put a tackle in, the ball had already been shifted. Then Brazil had a moment of madness on the 37th minute.

Midfielder Clodoaldo tried a ridiculous backheel in his own half when there was absolutely no need to do it. The ball was pinched off him by Boninsenga, who stumbled towards the goal, somehow managed to spin the 'keeper and bundled the ball into the empty net. The Brazil players looked stunned, but their casual approach to the game had backfired.

The teams went in at halftime with the score at 1–1. Despite Brazil's near-total dominance, Italy would have been the happier of the two simply because they could have been so far behind on another day.

Brazil came out for the second half with the same approach, only this time, there seemed to be a little more urgency to their play.

With 66 minutes played, Gérson picked the ball up just outside the box following another patient Brazil attack. He shifted his body once, gaining some space, then drilled a left-footed shot into the top corner. The celebrations felt more like relief than joy, and the boys from Brazil seemed to collectively exhale. Then they really turned on the style.

Their next goal came five minutes later when Pelé nodded a deep cross down into the path of Jairzinho, who tapped the ball into the net to make it 3-1. Their tails were up, and Italy didn't really get another sniff after that. In fact, they could only watch in awe like everyone else when Brazil got their fourth, a passing move that is widely regarded as the greatest team goal ever scored at a World Cup.

With four Italian players around him and deep in his own half, Clodoaldo —the player who had been at fault for Italy's goal—casually danced through every one of them before rolling the ball off to Rivellino, who had wandered over from the opposite wing. He took one touch and clipped the ball up the line to Jairzinho, and with a drop of the shoulder, he left another couple of Italian defenders chasing shadows. Jairzinho found Pelé just outside the box, who waited for his full-back to come up on his blind side before rolling it into his path. Carlos Alberto slammed the ball home to complete an incredible move, and the 4-1 rout was complete.

The move was indicative of how Brazil played the game. They would have to wait another 24 years before they lifted the trophy again, but their style and influence on future generations would last for eternity.

ITALY v BRAZIL

5th of July 1982
Second Round Group Stage
Estadio Sarriá, Barcelona, Spain
Attendance: 44,000

Brazil were heavy favourites coming into the last group game against Italy. Their passing style—a form of tika-taka before the term tika-taka existed—was beautiful to watch, but defensively, it was questioned by the purists. This World Cup was seen as the deciding factor in the age-old debate of whether playing pretty football could bring results or not.

Italy, on the other hand, were being eaten alive by the press back home due to their inclusion of Paulo Rossi in their squad. Although regarded as a top striker, he had only returned from a two-year ban for match-fixing a few weeks before the tournament in Spain began. When he failed to score in any of Italy's first four games, the media back in Italy were relentless.

The World Cup in '82 was a little different in that it had two group stages before the semis. In FIFA's eternity-long mission to fix what isn't broken, the new format meant that teams could play terribly, snatch a few draws, and still qualify from their group—something the Italians took full advantage of when they failed to win a game in the first section.

Three draws against Poland, Cameroon and Peru saw them only net twice and scrape through ahead of the Cameroonians due to goal difference. Even then, it was only goals scored that made the difference. Italy netted two in three matches while Cameroon only managed one. If it weren't for the likes of Dino Zoff in goal and Claudio Gentile at the back—plus the two points for a win rule—they would have gone home long before Pavarotti had sung.

Brazil were the chalk to Italy's cheese, winning all three matches and smashing home 10 goals in the process. Their silky stars, such as Zico, Sócrates and Falcão were having a field day, and it looked for all the world that the Brazilians would saunter to the trophy.

The second group stage consisted of three teams in each one, with Italy getting dumped in with Brazil and the holders, Argentina. Italy shocked the Argies with a 2-1 win in the first game, and Brazil thumped their fiercest rivals in the second. It all meant that Brazil could qualify for the semis with a draw, while Italy had to win.

The match took place in Espanyol's now-demolished stadium, the Estadio de Sarrià in Barcelona. With the sun beating down and 44,000 in attendance, fans around the world prepared for a footballing lesson to be handed down to the Italians. And that is how the game started.

Large parts of the match were spent with the Brazilians popping the ball around Italy's final third. Their pretty football breached the Azzurri's backline on occasion, but Dino Zoff was usually there to mop up any rare mistakes his solid defence made. Italy had planned to soak up the pressure and hit the Brazilians on the counterattack, but in truth, they had no other choice.

Paulo Rossi's name had been widely booed when the teams had been announced, and the displeasure at his inclusion, coupled with the nightmarish World Cup he'd had thus far, continued with his first few touches. But it soon turned to cheers when he headed in Antonio Cabrini's cross on five minutes, shocking the Brazilians and everyone watching.

Claudio Gentile had been deployed as a man-marker, with his instructions to stick to Zico like glue seeming to pay off early on. The Brazilian legend cut a frustrated figure as he tried to drop into little pockets of space, only to find a blue shirt merging with his yellow one. With Zico being taken out of the game, Brazil needed the rest of their players to step up. Thankfully for them, they had superstars in abundance.

The gangly figure of Sócrates ghosted through the Italian backline seven minutes after Rossi's goal to calmly slot the ball past Zoff. A sea of yellow celebrated, and the general feeling amongst the fans and commentators was that the floodgates were about to open and drench the Italians. They were wrong.

In the 25th minute, the Brazilians' need to move the ball around in front of their own goal proved devastating when Rossi sprinted in to nip the ball away and close in on goal. He calmly finished, wheeling away in delight as the Brazilian players looked for someone to blame. They quickly recovered, though, and began bombarding the Italian backline with wave after wave of silky attacks.

Falcão slammed the ball in from 20 yards with 25 minutes left to play, and the Italians were back to square one. In true Brazilian fashion, they continued to attack despite the fact they would go through if the score remained the same. Italy looked tired, but on the 76th minute, they won their first corner of the match. It was lumped in, and after a scramble around the six-yard box, the ball fell to Rossi, who squeezed it home to complete his hat trick.

Dino Zoff produced a world-class save in injury time to deny Oscar, and the Italians booked their place in the semifinal.

Amazingly, Rossi would go on to score twice more in the semi and again in the final, giving him the Golden Boot and Best Player of the Tournament awards. He would finish the year by being named as the winner of the Ballon d'Or, marking one of the greatest career turnarounds in sports history.

WEST GERMANY v FRANCE

8th of July 1982
Semi-final
Estadio Sarriá, Barcelona, Spain
Attendance: 44,000

The World Cup in '82 had already produced some of the most memorable moments in the history of football. The temperature had played a big part in making things even more tense by the time West Germany lined up against France in the semifinal in Seville. Most of the games—especially in Seville—had been arranged with a 9 p.m. kick-off to avoid the choking heat. Even so, the match between the Germans and the French saw temperatures in the high thirties.

France, like the silky Holland side of the 70s, were already getting a name as also-rans. It seemed that every tournament brought with it massive expectations and unanimous cries of "This has to be their year," yet they were still to reach their maiden final. The Germans had already lifted the trophy twice, in '54 and '74, and they were looking to make it three to tie themselves with the Brazilians for the most World Cups ever won.

West Germany came into the game as slight favourites, despite the mercurial Michel Platini leading the French side. Platini would follow the World Cup in '82 by winning the Ballon d'Or three times in a row, and his performance against the Germans on that muggy night in Seville is widely regarded as his most beautiful.

But the silky, swaggering skills of Platini would be overshadowed in a game that brought the first-ever penalty shoot-out in a World Cup and what can only be described as a case of grievous bodily harm involving the German 'keeper Harald Schumacher.

France's chances were strengthened when Germany's talisman, Karl-Heinz Rummenigge, was ruled out before kick-off with a hamstring injury. That year's European Footballer of the Year still took his place on the bench, though. In 1982, teams didn't bring squads of 30 with them to tournaments, and injured players were often considered for selection despite the pain they were in.

The French took the game to the Germans early on, but if history has taught us anything, that is often when Germany are at their most dangerous. In the 17th minute, French 'keeper Jean-Luc Ettori was caught daydreaming, and Klaus Fischer closed him down as he got caught in two minds. The ball squirmed into the path of Pierre Littbarski, and he slotted it home to give the Germans the lead.

Only 10 minutes later, German defender Bernd Forster pulled down Dominique Rocheteau in the box, and France were awarded a penalty. Michel Platini, his socks down, jersey out, and the iconic Number 10 on his back, stepped up to coolly stick the ball away. France were deservedly level, and they continued to pepper the German goal in search of a winner.

The first half ended with France on top, but the second period saw a revitalised Germany giving as good as they got. But the game was about to enter the realm of the ridiculous, and one of the most brutal tackles ever seen stained an otherwise beautiful match. With 55 minutes on the clock, French defender Patrick Battiston raced through on goal with only the 'keeper to beat. Unfortunately for him, that 'keeper was the moustachioed Harald Schumacher.

With no intention of getting to the ball, Schumacher charged from his goal and leapt into the air just as he neared Battiston. In the instant before they collided, the German turned his side to the onrushing Frenchman, slamming his hip into Battiston's face. The impact was horrendous, and the cameras zoomed in as the French player lay motionless on the turf for over five minutes.

It would later be revealed that Battiston lost two teeth, damaged his vertebrae, and fell into a coma following the collision. Amazingly, Dutch referee Charles Corver didn't send the smiling Schumacher off. In fact, he awarded Germany a goal kick.

In an interview after the game, Schumacher was informed about Battiston's condition. Upon hearing that the man he clattered into had, amongst other things, lost a couple of teeth, he replied, "If that's all that's wrong with him, I'll pay for his crowns" (Hannigan, 2020).

The rest of the 90 minutes played out at a slower pace. The long, drawn-out removal of Battiston from the pitch as the medics pumped oxygen into him had clearly rattled the players. Normal service resumed in extra time, though, with both teams having a real go.

Marius Trésor volleyed the ball home two minutes into the first period of extra time to put the French in front for the first time. Sensing the tide shifting, Germany sent on the injured Rummenigge in the hopes that he could spark them into life. It didn't initially work, and France went 3-1 up in the 98th minute. Germany looked beaten, and it seemed like Platini and the boys in blue were already making plans for the final in the Bernabéu in three days' time.

Just before the end of the first half of extra time, Rummenigge slotted home coolly with the outside of his foot to give the Germans hope. In fact, there was suddenly an air of inevitability that the team that had looked down and out less than 10 minutes before would equalise. They did so when Fischer sent the German crowd wild with a stunning bicycle kick with 12 minutes remaining.

The game ended 3-3, and the first-ever penalty shoot-out in World Cup history played out. Germany, who would make a habit of dominating that format, won the shoot-out 5-4 in sudden death. They would go on to the final to face an Italy side that had shocked the world by beating Brazil in the quarterfinals, with both teams looking for that elusive third World Cup.

The game that became known as the unimaginative "Night in Seville" will always be remembered for Schumacher's horror tackle, but there was some astronomical football on display too. Also, the Germans got a taste of their first penalty shoot-out, which turned out to be bad news for the rest of the footballing world.

SOVIET UNION v BELGIUM

15th of June 1986
Round of 16
Estadio Nou Camp, León, Mexico
Attendance: 32,277

Both sides had met in the previous World Cup's group stage, a 1-0 win for the Soviets at the Nou Camp in Spain. When they faced off again in 1986, it was again at the Nou Camp, only this time the Estadio Nou Camp in León, Guanajuato. Unlike the drab affair in Spain in 1982, this one would be an absolute cracker.

The World Cup in '86 was probably when football went from being huge to globally astronomical. It was when Panini stickers were all the rage, and players from nations and leagues that had only ever been read about in magazines were all broadcast live and in colour. It was glamorous and magical, and the vast number of different nations from further than ever added an aura of a genuine worldwide battle to be the best.

The USSR had fared well throughout the eighties, and it seemed like something special was happening with the national team. Whether World Cup '86 came a little too soon, we'll never know, but the Soviets would go on to claim gold at the Olympics in 1988 and just lose the European Championship Final to a van Basten-inspired Holland side.

Belgium had only barely gotten out of their group as one of the few third-placed teams with three points. The USSR, on the other hand, had topped their group unbeaten, thrashing Hungary 6-0 along the way. By the time the team buses had pulled up outside the Estadio Nou Camp León, the Soviets were by far the heavy favourites. Football doesn't always play out as it should, though, and the USSR were about to find that out the hard way.

The Soviets had included Igor Belanov in the starting 11, a man who had only played four games for his country before the World Cup, failing to score in all of them. His inclusion was looked upon with significant scepticism, but he had started the tournament well, and his rising form would continue into the last 16 tie against the Belgians.

The game kicked off at 16:00, under the glaring Mexican sun, and neither team were adept at playing in such conditions. Still, it was felt that the Soviets would handle it better, given the preparation they'd been given under the guidance of the USSR coach and trailblazer Valeriy Lobanovskyi. Fearing a Soviet onslaught, Belgium started the game with only Jan Ceulemans up front in an attempt to pack the midfield and suffocate their creative opponents.

Belgium's plans were shattered after 27 minutes when Belanov scored a cracker from just outside the box, taking the ball in his stride before smashing it into the top corner. The USSR sat back for a while after that, letting the Belgians have a bit of the ball as they tried to pick them off on the counter. Despite some decent Belgian chances, the score remained 1-0 at halftime.

It felt like the second half might play out the same way, and no more goals would have been a sound bet to make if you were that way inclined. But Belgian wonder kid Enzo Scifo hadn't read the script, and he popped up at the back post in the 53rd minute to coolly slot the ball home. Belgium celebrated, and the USSR knew they needed to open up once more if they were to win the game.

They began to retake control, and in the 70th minute, Belgian captain Jan Ceulemans was caught dallying on the ball. He quickly disposed of it, and the ball found its way to Belanov, who tucked it away with another superb finish to make it 2-1. The man who the Soviet fans had demanded not even be on the plane to Mexico was proving all of his doubters wrong.

Belgium came right back at them, and it only took another seven minutes before they were level again. After some slow build-up, the Belgium midfield struggled to pick out a pass of any real meaning. The Soviets had parked the bus, and in the end, Stéphane Demol—being heavily pressured by Belanov—was forced to hoof the ball the of the field. Jan Ceulemans latched onto it and calmly stroked the ball into the net to make up for his earlier mistake.

The Soviet players screamed for offside, and the linesman on the far side actually raised his flag. Amazingly, the referee ignored his assistant, and the goal stood. Belgium had equalised, and they kept it that way until the end of the 90 minutes.

This game went from being a cracker to an all-time classic in extra time, and the thunderstorm that had just broken out in the skies above seemed to mirror what was taking place on the pitch. Both teams lost the plot a little, and the match became a frantic blow-for-blow encounter that seemed to promise a goal with every attack. Belgium struck first, with Stéphane Demol heading in a well-worked corner with 102 minutes played. It was the first time Belgium had the lead in this enthralling encounter.

Both teams looked shattered, and after some lacklustre attempts at clearing the ball following a Belgium corner, substitute striker Nico Claesen scored to send the Belgians into dreamland. The unthinkable suddenly looked very real for the first time, but the USSR rallied nonetheless.

From kick-off, they charged forward, loading as many men into the Belgian half as they could muster. It paid off, and only a minute after Belgium's fourth goal, the USSR were awarded a penalty. Belanov stepped up and absolutely rammed the ball into the net to complete his hat trick. The Soviets fought until the end, but the damage had already been done, and they crashed out before the quarters.

Igor Belanov's impressive performances earned him the European Player of the Year award in '86, but his four goals and six assists in the World Cup weren't enough to stop his side from going out. Belgium became a true surprise package when they went on to beat Spain on penalties in the next round but came unstuck in the semis when Diego Maradona ripped them to shreds. It was Belgium's best performance in a major tournament until the golden age of 2018, and for the USSR, they had to regroup and concentrate on the upcoming Euros in '88.

ARGENTINA v ENGLAND

22nd of June 1986

Quarter-final

Estadio Azteca, Mexico City, Mexico

Attendance: 114,580

Although the English and Argentine players had come out in the lead up to the game and informed the press that the Falklands War was the furthest thing from their thoughts, it still hung over the game like a dark cloud. Diego Maradona was in the prime of his career, and the barrel-chested magician had gone against the grain and openly admitted that the match was all about revenge.

England had come into the tournament amidst the mess of destruction and violence of football hooliganism that had dominated the 80s and left a stain on the reputation of their fan base. On the pitch, the highs of '66 had long faded, and two decades had passed since the last time they tasted glory. Argentina had limped out of the '82 World Cup having relinquished the crown they'd earned four years earlier, and Maradona seemed obsessed with regaining what he felt was his birthright.

With all of the ingredients boiling over even before a ball had been kicked, one of the greatest matches in footballing history was ready to unfold.

The heat inside the Aztec Stadium in Mexico City was relentless as the players lined up for the national anthems. England had openly spoken of the dangers of Diego Maradona, and the man himself had already shredded every team that had been put in front of him in their group, helping Argentina top it. On the other hand, England had scraped through a relatively easy group on goal difference, and the press back home were already sharpening their knives.

In a match that would produce possibly the two most famous moments in World Cup history, the player who would create both started the game like a man possessed. The English players couldn't get near Maradona as he wove his way through the team with ease. The hard-hitting tight marking that had battered Diego out of the '82 World Cup had forced FIFA to impose stricter rules on defenders who used excessive force. Given more freedom to operate, Maradona was Given more freedom to operate, Maradona was almost unplayable that summer in Mexico.

The opening stages of the match saw Argentina dominate, and England's 'keeper, Peter Shilton, had to pull off several top-class saves. England had some superstars of their own to depend on, with the likes of Glenn Hoddle, Peter Beardsley and eventual Golden Boot winner Gary Lineker posing a real threat going forward. The only problem seemed to be getting the ball off Argentina's Number 10 long enough to do something about it.

Despite Argentina's dominance, the sides went in goalless at halftime. But the heat was clearly affecting the English players more, and their opponents always looked like they had a couple of more gears to go up if needed. They did in the second half, and the goal that opened the scoring instantly became an eternal pop culture image around the world and a 24/7 news story in Britain for many months after.

With six minutes of the second half played, Maradona tried to play a one-two with teammate Jorge Valdano. The return pass was deflected and spun up into the air, with the little Argentinian maestro continuing his run into the box. Shilton came to claim a ball that, in all fairness, he should have caught despite what followed, and Maradona rose to punch the ball into the empty net.

As he wheeled away in celebration, the incredulous English players surrounded the ref. It was clear to everyone watching what had happened, but the goal stood, and the infamous "Hand of God" moment was forever etched in football's history. England never really recovered, but if Maradona's first goal was the man at his worst, then the one that followed was the side of him that made miracles happen on the pitch.

Only four minutes after cheating the English, Maradona picked the ball up in his own half and spun Peter Beardsley. Accelerating, he ghosted by the flailing Peter Reid and Terry Butcher, leaving them visibly bamboozled. As Diego slowed his pace for a split second, Butcher recovered some ground, only to be mugged off again as the little Argentinian slipped by him with ease. Shilton came out to try to smother the ball but was rounded too before Maradona slotted the ball home with the outside of his left peg.

This time when the goalscorer wheeled away, nobody complained. To the 114,580 people in the Azteca, the players on the pitch, and the millions watching at home, something truly phenomenal had just occurred. Maradona's solo effort was soon dubbed the "Goal of the Century," and rightly so. It is still regularly named number one on most people's Greatest Goals of All Time lists and was worthy of winning any match.

England dusted themselves off and admirably launched a wave of attacks in an attempt to narrow the deficit. They brought on Chris Waddle and the fantastic John Barnes in a do-or-die move that nearly paid off. In fact, it was Barnes's wizardry on the wing that set up Lineker's goal—his sixth in four games—in the 86th minute. Despite both teams continuing to attack, the game ended 2-1 to Argentina.

The England team returned home to heavy criticism. The flair being shown by the likes of Platini and Maradona in the 80s had changed the face of football. No longer could teams survive with two speedy wingers lumping balls into the box. The classic Number 10 and slick passing had overtaken the old way for a long time already, and many England fans felt like the football they had invented was being left behind.

As for Maradona and Argentina, they would go on to lift the trophy. A rivalry with England that had only been a seed before the Azteca encounter had fully germinated and grown to Jack and the Beanstalk proportions. They would have many more battles in the future, but '86 will always be remembered for the Hand of God and the Goal of the Century.

ARGENTINA v ENGLAND

30th of June 1998

Round of 16

Stade Geoffroy-Guichard, Saint-Étienne,
France

Attendance: 30,600

A classic rivalry needs a classic encounter, and the match between Argentina and England in Saint-Étienne in '98 was all of that and more. Both sides hadn't met competitively since Maradona's Hand of God and Goal of the Century exploits in '86, and the tensions created that night seemed to have not deteriorated at all by the time the sides faced each other in their last 16 clash.

Maradona was gone, but the Argies still boasted the likes of Gabriel Batistuta, Ariel Ortega and Diego Simeone, the latter of whom would be involved in one of the more controversial moments during the match. England had performed well enough, with a mixture of experience and youth making them look like a threat to anyone when they clicked. David Beckham and an 18-year-old Michael Owen had spent the first couple of group games on the bench, but their wonderful performances, when called upon, had forced manager Glenn Hoddle to include them from the start in the knockout stage.

For one of them, it would be the moment he set the world alight. For the other, the only things being set on fire would be the effigies of him following a rush of blood to the head that would haunt him for years.

Argentina had been drawn as the home side, even though both teams were technically away. Instead of wearing their classic baby blue and white striped kits, the players decided to use their navy away jerseys, much like they had in '86. Under the floodlights of the Stade Geoffroy-Guichard, and with just over 30,000 supporters crammed into the ground, two of international football's fiercest foes prepared to do battle.

England started with the wily Alan Shearer partnering the electric Michael Owen up front. It was a frontline any team in the world would envy, and they took the game to the Argentinians from the first whistle. Their overly intense start proved to be their undoing, though, and in Argentina's first real attack of note, the English defence were caught napping.

In only the sixth minute, Batistuta played a quick through ball to Simeone, who expertly drew the foul from England 'keeper David Seaman. The ref gave the penalty, which still wasn't enough for Simeone, who dramatically waved an imaginary card in the official's face in an attempt to get Seaman sent off. It didn't work, and after a slight delay, Batistuta tucked the penalty into the corner. Seaman got a good hand to it, but it wasn't enough to stop Argentina from going 1-0 up.

Three minutes later, it was Michael Owen dropping to the deck in the Argentinian's box. Again, the referee pointed to the spot. It was a weak penalty to give, but England would have felt it was justified after Simeone's shenanigans moments before. Alan Shearer dispatched the penalty with ease, slamming it into the top corner to give Carlos Roa no chance. The Argentinian goalie who would retire to a turnip farm a year later at the age of 30 because he believed the world was going to end couldn't get near the ball, and he would soon pick it out of the net once more when one of the competition's greatest-ever goals was scored.

With still only 16 minutes on the clock, Michael Owen was played through by Beckham just past the halfway line. Despite his small stature, the wonder kid shrugged off a few defenders before putting on the afterburners and leaving them in his dust. As the advancing Carlos Roa tried to close him down, Owen clipped the ball into the top corner without breaking his stride. It was a rapid turnaround by the English, but unfortunately for them, it didn't last too long.

An expertly worked free kick just outside the England penalty box saw their defence look confused as a disguised pass found its way to Javier Zanetti just inside the area. He drove it into the net to send the Argentinians wild, and England were left reeling on the stroke of halftime. It was a devastating blow, and the aftershock of the goal bled through into the second period. In fact, it only took two minutes of the second half for England—and especially a young David Beckham—to implode.

After a coming together with Argentina's mercurial huckster Simeone, Beckham ended up on the deck. In a moment of madness that he would forever regret, he flung a boot up at his sneaky opponent. The connection he made was minimal at best, but Simeone went down like he had been taken out by a sniper's bullet. The ref bought it and sent Beckham off. In the months and years that followed, the England fans treated Beckham horrifically, and stuffed dummies of him being set on fire at football grounds around the country was not an uncommon sight.

Now that England were down to 10 men, they needed to reorganise. They switched to a slightly more conservative approach and allowed their opponents to have most of the ball in the hope that they could catch them on the counter. They still had Owen up front, and his pace had already scared the life out of Argentina. After the end-to-end affair in the first half, things became a lot nervier for both sides as the game wore on. England had chances, but the Argies controlled the rest of the game for long periods without ever really coming very close. It was actually England who should have won it when Sol Campbell's 81st-minute header was wrongfully disallowed for a foul that never happened.

The game went to extra time, and it became more of a case of who didn't want to make a mistake. Penalties seemed the most likely outcome, and they were to be England's downfall yet again. Only two years before, they had suffered the same fate against their other rivals, Germany, in the semifinals of the Euros. The cries of "Football's Coming Home" and the image of a forlorn Gareth Southgate must have been all the players could envision as they stepped up to the spot yet again in '98.

Although Seaman saved Argentina's second penalty, Paul Ince fluffed his lines before David Batty stepped up and weakly prodded the ball down Roa's throat. It was heartbreak again for England, and they walked off feeling rightly aggrieved at the referee. It was yet another hard-to-swallow case of "what if." Argentina would go out in the next round thanks to Dennis Bergkamp's genius goal in the last minute of their quarterfinal clash. For England, it was back to the drawing board yet again. They had the players capable of winning a major tournament, but it seemed that something impossible to pinpoint was always missing.

ITALY v FRANCE

9th of July 2006
Final
Olympiastadion, Berlin, Germany
Attendance: 69,000

Another one of world football's fiercest rivalries is that of Italy and France. In fact, Italy's first-ever official match in 1910 was against the French, and ever since, they have often found themselves facing each other in major tournaments. When they faced each other in 2006, the Euro 2000 final was still fresh in everyone's mind. France won that 2-1 with a golden goal in extra time from David Trezeguet after Alessandro Del Piero had missed a stream of chances to put the Italians out of reach.

When they met in the 2006 showpiece, Italy were hunting for their fourth World Cup, which would have put them one ahead of Germany and one behind Brazil. France had lifted their first in 1998, and they were looking to get their second that evening in Berlin.

Much of the talk before the game had surrounded the imminent retirement of Zinedine Zidane, and the final was set as his last game as a professional. The whole thing felt like a Roy of the Rovers comic, with a script seemingly being written for the France captain to lift the trophy and walk off into the sunset. He had every chance to, as the French possessed some of the greatest players on the planet.

Italy lined up with Luca Toni leading the line, with Francesco Totti just behind. They had Fabio Cannavaro in defence, a man who would finish that year winning the Ballon d'Or, which is unheard of for a centre-back. With Gattuso and Pirlo in central midfield, Italy were a match for anyone and had proved this by getting to the final, having conceded just one goal along the way.

France had scraped through one of the weakest groups in World Cup history, bumbling past Togo, Switzerland and South Korea before finishing second. It was these performances that made their journey through the knockout phase all the more surprising, as they beat Spain, Brazil and Portugal to book their place in the final. Despite their early performances, France were a lot of people's favourite before kick-off. Apart from Zidane, they boasted the likes of Theirry Henry, Patrick Vieira and Lilian Thuram, to name but a few. It was seen as France's attacking flair against Italy's solid defence, although what the fans were given was an end-to-end classic with one of the competition's most controversial and famous moments to top it off.

Amazingly, the 2006 final was the first in 20 years where both teams scored, and they did so in the first 19 minutes. Even more bizarrely, both were scored by the two players who would become entangled in that incident at the end.

The first goal came from a penalty after only seven minutes when Florent Malouda went down under a challenge from Marco Materazzi. Zinedine Zidane took the spot kick, casually chipping a Panenka down the centre of the goal. There was a moment as it hit the bar when it looked like his arrogance had backfired, but it clipped the underside and dropped into the goal at the last moment.

Italy responded well, popping the ball around the pitch in an effort to slow down France's momentum. They were awarded a corner in the 19th minute, and Pirlo whipped in a beauty that was met by Marco Materazzi, who headed it into the net. Italy continued to press, and another Pirlo corner found the head of Luca Toni 20 minutes later, only this time, the resulting header rebounded back off the bar.

The second half mainly belonged to France, and they had several chances that Gianluigi Buffon handled impeccably. The Italian goalkeeper will always be regarded as one of the best of all time in his position, and he proved it time and again that night in Berlin. Malouda also had another penalty claim, but the ref waved it away.

Italy created chances of their own, but they were few and far between. However, they did have a goal disallowed in the 62nd minute when Luca Toni's forehead met yet another Pirlo set piece. The ball hit the net, but as the Italians celebrated, the linesman raised his flag and it was ruled out for offside.

Extra time saw Buffon at his best once more, miraculously tipping a

Zidane header onto the bar in the 105th minute. Italy were now playing backs-to-the-wall football, but as we've seen throughout history, that can be when they are at their most effective. It is usually during these moments when the Italian mind games start, and five minutes after Zidane used his head to direct the ball onto Buffon's hand, he was using it again, but for completely different reasons.

After another French attack had been broken up by the gritty Italian defence, Zidane and Materazzi had a bit of a coming together off the ball. It looked like nothing and the type of back-and-forth that happens all the time during a game. As Zidane jogged away from Materazzi, the Italian shouted something offensive. In a moment of sheer madness, Zidane marched back towards the Italian and laid him out with a powerful headbutt to the chest.

Materazzi collapsed to the ground in a heap, of course, and when Zidane was shown the red card, he didn't even argue his case. He was bang to rights, and it would take months for the truth to come out about what provoked the usually calm Frenchman to react in such a way. When it did, most people took Zidane's side, but the fact remained that he had fallen for Materazzi's mind games and let his team down. According to Materazzi, after over 100 minutes of him slyly tugging at Zidane's shirt, the Frenchman said, "If you want it so much, I'll give it to you after the game," to which Materazzi shouted, "I prefer the whore that is your sister" (Sidle, 2020).

The match fizzled out after the red card, and both nations played like two teams accepting that the game was going to penalties, which it did. David Trezeguet, who had scored the golden goal winner against Italy six years earlier, was the only player to miss his spot kick. Fabio Grosso blasted home Italy's fifth penalty to send the nation wild. As they all ran towards the goal scorer to embrace him, Zinedine Zidane must have been wondering how things might have turned out if he'd still been on the pitch to take one of France's penalties.

Alas, his last action in a football shirt was headbutting Marco Materazzi.

URUGUAY v GHANA

2nd of July 2010
Quarter-final
Soccer City, Johannesburg, South Africa
Attendance: 84,017

Amazingly, this would be the first time that these two nations met each other in a competitive fixture. The Uruguayans had only conceded one goal in their opening four matches, whereas the Ghanaians had wowed the world with their powerful attacks and fluid football. It would prove to be an extraordinary clash of styles that epitomises everything that is great about international football.

The World Cup in South Africa had been a bit stop-starty throughout. The incessant noise of thousands of vuvuzelas being blown endlessly during every match had started to grate on the nerves of fans and players alike, with several of the latter openly complaining about it. Still, the event proved to be an entertaining one in the end for several reasons, and the clash between two-time champions Uruguay and every football fan's preference—Ghana—produced some of the more memorable moments.

Uruguay had topped a group that had included France and Mexico without conceding, and after getting a scare in their last 16 clash with South Korea, felt ready to push on a challenge for a World Cup for the first time in 60 years. With Diego Forlán and Luiz Suárez up front, they would always be in with a chance. Having solidified their defence and ironed out most of the disciplinary problems that had let them down in the past, there was a genuine feeling that they could go all the way with a bit of luck.

For Ghana, the group stage had been a little trickier, and it had taken goal difference for them to scrape through after a win, a loss and a draw. After disposing of the United States in the last 16, they felt they were ready to go one further than the Roger Milla- inspired Cameroonian side of Italia '90 and become the first African side in history to reach the semifinal of a World Cup. If it weren't for the hand of one Mr Suárez, they probably would have.

The first half saw Uruguay dominate, with quick, aggressive counterattacks from the Ghanaians peppered in between. When Uruguayan captain and rock Diego Lugan limped off with only 38 minutes played, Ghana switched it up and caught their opponents off guard. With the first half drifting into injury time, Sulley Muntari picked the ball up 40 yards from goal and looked for runners. It seemed like there was no danger until he let fly with a rocket that left Uruguay's 'keeper Fernando Muslera helpless.

It was a devastating blow for Uruguay and a horrible way to end a first half they mainly controlled. Still, they had Suárez and Forlán in attack, and the latter slapped in a free kick on 55 minutes to level the score. It felt like Uruguay would seize the momentum, but instead, the game became a breath-taking end-to-end affair that seemed to play out in fast forward. Both teams had chances, but the game went to extra time in the end with the score 1–1.

It was during this period that one of the most controversial players in recent history created yet another addition to his Greatest Hits. As extra time drew to a close and both teams psyched themselves up for penalties, Ghana won a free kick just outside the Uruguayan box. The ball was swung in from the right, and Fernando Muslera flapped at it. In the impending scramble, the ball fell to Stephen Appiah, but his six-yard effort was blocked on the line by Suárez. Then all hell broke loose.

As the ball looped up in the air from Suárez's initial block, Ghanain striker Dominic Adiyiah rose highest to head it back at goal. Suárez blocked it again, only this time with his hand, much to the fervent protests of the Ghanaian players. It was a decade before VAR, but the ref could have seen the incident through fogged-up glasses and figured out what happened.

Suárez was sent off and left the field in tears, and as Ghana's star man Asamoah Gyan placed the ball down on the penalty spot, it looked for all the world like his nation was about to make history and qualify for the semis. With the clock in the process of ticking into the 120th minute, a goal surely would have been enough to send Ghana through.

Gyan smashed the ball off the bar, much to the delight of Suárez, who celebrated like crazy on the touchline. He later claimed that he "made the save of the tournament" and that The Hand of God now belonged to him. Many people saw his handball as the lowest form of cheating, but in a sport where overpaid players seem to disgrace themselves in their personal lives on a daily basis, I think we can put it a little nicer and say he took one for the team.

The penalty shoot-out that followed soon after felt like an afterthought. Suárez's actions were still too fresh in everyone's mind.

It was Diego Forlan, winner of the Golden Ball at the tournament, who stepped up first, duly sending the keeper the wrong way. Next, it was that man Gyan again just moments after his heartbreaking miss in extra time. This time he scored an inch-perfect penalty into the top corner which gave the keeper no chance despite going the right way. The next three penalties were scored until Ghana's captain saw his tame effort saved by Fernando Muslera.

After another Ghanainin miss, it was up to the man nicknamed Loco (meaning madman) Sebastián Abreu to send Uruguay into the last 4. He certainly lived up to that name as he proceeded to produce a panenka straight down the middle as the hapless Richard Kingson dived to his right. It was that kick that bought an end to the Ghanaian's incredible adventure.

Uruguay would get no further than the semifinals and then lose the third place playoff to Germany a week after Suárez's controversial handball. As it turned out, his sacrifice was in vain, but it did raise an often-debated question: At what point does taking one for the team become downright cheating?

For the man who would go on to take lumps out of a couple of players with his bare teeth, a handball in injury time must have felt like his most honourable moment to date.

SPAIN v NETHERLANDS

13th of June 2014
Group Stage
Itaipava Arena Fonte Nova, Salvador, Brazil
Attendance: 48,173

Seeing the defending champions slip up in the opening game of a World Cup isn't an anomaly. In fact, it can be quite a common occurrence, truth be told. Think Argentina losing to nine-man Cameroon in 1990 or France being completely outplayed by Senegal in 2002, and you will be somewhere in the ballpark of what happened to Spain on 13 June 2014 in Bahia, Brazil. The two aforementioned results had been shocks; what happened to Spain was in the realm of unthinkable.

Spain had come into the 2014 tournament not only as defending champions but as double European Championship Winners too. Sure, their team had aged a little, but they still began the 2014 tournament as favourites. The Dutch had lost to the Spaniards in that 2010 final, and it was felt by most that the same result would probably be the outcome once more, despite some real stars in the Holland team.

The Spanish team around that time was considered by many to be the greatest there had ever been. They had style, class and talent in abundance, but a few cracks were starting to appear in the Rolls-Royce exterior. For one thing, the players were getting older, and like all good things, it had to come to an end sooner or later. The biggest shock was actually how spectacularly it came crashing down that day in Brazil.

For most fans and pundits, the 2014 Holland team was actually weaker than the one that had come so close four years before in South Africa. Spain had lost a little of their edge, too, but they still possessed players like Xavi, Sergio Busquets and Iker Casillas. As far as opening group games go, this one was a glamour tie of the highest calibre, and it is actually the only time that two previous finalists have met at that stage in a World Cup.

Spain started the brighter of the two, which makes what happened later in the game so much harder to comprehend. When Diego Costa flopped to the ground inside the box on 26 minutes, and the ref somehow pointed to the spot, Xabi Alonso stepped up and calmly slotted the resulting penalty kick home. The Spanish crowd celebrated, and it seemed like normal service had been resumed, but things went in a whole other direction.

Holland had Arjen Robben and captain Robin van Persie up front, and both were in their prime around 2014. And van Persie scored the tournament's best goal just before the stroke of halftime when Daley Blind spotted him making a run into the box and picked him out with a 50-yard pass. Unable to take the ball down due to the trajectory, van Persie magically adjusted his body mid-stride and threw himself into a diving header. He connected perfectly, looping the ball over the stranded Casillas.

It was a big blow for the Spaniards, who had hoped to go in at halftime with the lead intact. Things got worse in the second period when Robben made it 2-1 with yet another assist from Blind. Spain tried to rally, but the Dutch had the bit between their teeth. It became one of those periods in football that come around every so often when a team just clicks, and every pass, shot and decision they attempt comes off.

Spain tried to deal with wave after wave of fluid Holland attacks, but there was an air of inevitability that 3-1 was only a matter of time in coming. It took another 12 minutes in the end when Dutch defender Stefan de Vrij nodded in Wesley Sneijder's free kick. Casillas protested that he had been impeded by van Persie, but it was all a little desperate. Holland's revenge would have been sweet if the game had ended then, but there was still much more to come.

With 72 minutes on the clock, Casillas's nightmare game got worse when van Persie stole the ball off him and tucked it away into an empty net to make it 4-1. Spain were in ribbons, and it was clear that their opponents were having a great time shredding them.

Throughout history, the Dutch national side has had a habit of shooting themselves in the foot just as everything looks hunky dory, but they stuck to the task and more that afternoon.

The fifth and final nail in the Spanish coffin came courtesy of Robben, and it was nearly as sublime as the first. In fact, if van Persie's header hadn't been so genius in its originality, then Robben's effort would have been a good shout for the goal of the tournament instead. When he picked the ball up in his own half, Robben had plenty of work left to do. Effortlessly, he left Sergio Ramos chasing shadows before slipping by a tired-looking Jordi Alba and calmly slotting the ball past Casillas to complete the rout.

As the Dutch players celebrated on the pitch after the final whistle, the Spaniards slunk off with their heads hung. It was a body blow they never recovered from, and like France in 2002, the defending champions failed to get out of their group. Holland would go on to the latter stages once more, but they inevitably ended up writing yet another chapter in the How Have They Never Won It? anthology that belongs solely to them.

The Spanish team that had dominated world football for three tournaments began to gradually lose its edge following the World Cup in 2014. They were still a force to be reckoned with but would never again get close to the phenomenal team many consider the greatest international side of all time.

BRAZIL v GERMANY

8th of July 2014
Semi-final
Estádio Mineirão, Belo Horizonte, Brazil
Attendance: 58,141

In 1950, when the Brazilian team shuffled out of the Maracanã following the shock 2-1 loss to Uruguay, it was felt that in terms of embarrassments on their own patch, they would never experience anything as bad. Of course, that was before Germany came to town in the summer of 2014 and flipped everything Brazil thought they knew about football on its head.

There has always been a rivalry between Brazil and Germany, but never a nasty one. A genuine appreciation for each nation's achievements has been long-standing, and by the time they met in that year's semifinal, both teams had shared eight World Cups between them, with Brazil having taken a record five and Germany three.

The game in Estadio Mineirão won't just be remembered because of the scoreline, as staggering as it ended up. It was also an evening when several long-standing records were broken and set, but unfortunately for the hosts, few were favourable to them.

Brazil came into the game against Germany having lost star player and professional tumbler Neymar to injury in the previous round. To make matters worse, their best defender Thiago Silva picked up a yellow card in the same game, meaning he was banned for the semi. Still, most pundits and fans alike expected a close affair, especially with Brazil having the home advantage.

Both sides had topped their respective groups with seven points but equally struggled in the first knockout game against weaker opposition. Brazil needed penalties to get past Chile, while Algeria took Germany to extra time in their clash. The quarterfinals brought out the best in both teams, though, with Brazil knocking out a strong Colombian side and the Germans beating France.

Both nations had previously met in the 2002 final, when one of Germany's weaker generations of players were soundly beaten by a Ronaldo (R9), Ronaldinho and Rivaldo- inspired Brazilian side. That result had given

Brazil their fifth World Cup and a bit of breathing room in the all-time tournament winners list, putting them two ahead of the Germans. This semifinal was seen as a massively important chapter in the story of arguably international football's two most successful sides.

In the end, it wasn't even a contest.

Well, it was for the first 10 minutes, and Brazil actually created quite a few chances early on. As each team counterattacked the other, everyone watching would have been forgiven if they had foreseen a tightly knit affair, even when Germany took the lead in the 11th minute through Thomas Müller. The German stalwart connected with a sweet Toni Kroos corner to side-foot the ball into the net, but only after some comical defending from David Luiz—the bumbling yet always entertaining Brazilian "defender."

The hosts had another 10-minute flurry where they tried in vain to create some chances. Germany repelled them pretty easily and then struck again in the 23rd minute through Miroslav Klose. Müller and Kroos combined again before setting up the German scoring legend to net his 16th World Cup goal in all competitions. Ironically, he overtook Ronaldo, the man who had scored both goals in the 2002 final to deny Klose's Germany.

After that, Brazil imploded. For anyone who has seen the game or even gone onto YouTube for the highlights, it is genuinely hard to watch. It seemed that every minute, David Luiz was picking the ball out of his own net.

Sixty seconds after Klose's goal, Kroos got his first of the match with sweetly struck left-footed effort. Brazil trundled back to the halfway line and kicked off again, only for Kroos to nick the ball off Fernandinho, play a one-two with Sami Khedira, and slot the ball past Julio Cesar. There had been just 69 seconds between both of his goals.

Khedira then got in on the action himself, latching onto a Mesut Özil pass to make it 5-0 to the Germans. The Brazilians were in total shock, and the stadium had become eerily quiet in the melee. There were moments when the camera would zoom in on the German players, and their expressions actually seemed to portray pity. In the space of six minutes, Germany had stuffed four past their opponents and went in 5-0 up at halftime.

The second half brought more of the same, although not at such intensity. Brazil created a few chances, and after removing the proverbial show pony Hulk during the break, there seemed to be a slight bit of solidity to their team. Their mini-revival lasted until the 69th minute when substitute André Schürrle stroked home a Philipp Lahm cross to make it 6-0. He added his second and Germany's seventh 10 minutes later with a cracking effort that might well have been the best of the bunch.

The Brazil fans that still remained in the stadium stood up and applauded the seventh goal and Germany's performance as a whole, which would have been the biggest insult of all for the Brazilian players. Oscar scored possibly the most meaningless goal in World Cup history when he pulled one back for Brazil in the 90th minute, but by that stage, his country's most humiliating result had already been inflicted.

The gulf in scores equalled Brazil's largest loss (6-0 to Uruguay in 1920), and it was also their first competitive defeat at home since 1975 when they lost to Peru in the Copa América.

Amazingly, they lost another record that night when Germany overtook them to become the highest-scoring nation in World Cup history. Brazil left the field in tears, the sounds of jeers and whistles echoing in their ears as they slipped away down the tunnel. For Germany, the only fear was that complacency might creep in before the final against old foes Argentina. It didn't, and Germany went on to lift their fourth World Cup, putting them only one behind the nation they had just humiliated in their own backyard.

BELGIUM v JAPAN

2nd of July 2018
Round of 16
Rostov Arena, Rostov-on-Don, Russia
Attendance: 41,466

The 2018 World Cup in Russia saw the introduction of VAR at that level. It also saw the nations of Iceland and Panama making their first appearances. On top of that, only 20 of the 32 teams from the previous World Cup in Brazil returned, proving that global football was no longer reserved for the same old big nations and their usual supporting cast. Now, previously perceived non-footballing countries were growing in stature.

Japan and Belgium were two of those nations who had become forces to be reckoned with in their own right. The Belgians were in the middle of their golden generation, with players like De Bruyne, Eden Hazard, Romelu Lukaku and Thibaut Courtois all coming through at the same time. In fact, they were ranked number one in the world before the tournament began, despite having not really won anything of note.

Japan had come through a tricky group and finished second behind Colombia. With attacking players like Honda, Osako and Kagawa to call on, they posed a threat to most teams. With their superb organisation and determination, they were undoubtedly one of the second-placed teams that the group winners were hoping to avoid in the first knockout stage.

Belgium had been rampant in the group stage, beating England, Tunisia and Panama. They came into the match against Japan as heavy favourites, and with their slick passing combined with the dribbling skills of players like Eden Hazard (before he went to Real Madrid and turned to mush), they were a lot of people's pick to go all the way.

The game kicked off in the Rostov Arena at night, with the floodlights illuminating the perfect pitch as the players lined up for the national anthems. Japan were the only Asian team left in the competition, and their fans had turned out in numbers, creating a wonderful atmosphere in the stadium as two teams who play football the right way prepared to go head-to-head.

The first half was a bit cagey, with both sides feeling each other out.

Although there was some excellent football, nobody could have predicted how the second period would go.

Still, both teams created chances, with Belgium having the better of them. Lukaku kept finding pockets of space in the Japanese box but just couldn't find the right connection to add the final touch. Japan hit Belgium on the break, happy enough to sit back and let their more skilful opponents have more of the ball.

The second half took only three minutes to burst into life. Belgian defender Jan Vertonghen mistimed an interception that he should have made, and the ball broke through for the onrushing Haraguchi. He took it in his stride before advancing on the Belgian goal and catching Courtois out with a snapshot into the bottom corner, leaving the pre-game favourites Belgium reeling.

Japan didn't sit back and took advantage of their clearly shell-shocked opponents. After an almost immediate reply from Belgium—when Hazard crashed his effort off the post—Japan stepped up a gear and took advantage of the evident self-pity that had befallen the Belgians.

Only four minutes after Japan had taken the lead, they struck again. Kagawa tried to find some space to work his magic outside the Belgian box, but nothing opened up. When he laid the ball off to Inui, it looked like they would have to go back to square one and start the move again. Inui had other ideas, and he took one touch to set himself before crashing the ball into the corner of the net from 20 yards out to send the Japanese supporters wild.

Belgium were in tatters, and it looked for all the world that they had seen the last 16 clash against Japan as nothing more than a formality that needed to be casually dealt with before they got to the real competition. The World Cup doesn't work like that, and almost every team can beat anyone else on their day.

The Belgians rallied, but it wasn't until the 69th minute that they got their reward. From a deep cross into the Japanese box, Jan Vertonghen looped a massive header back across the goal that dipped into the far corner of the net. Whether he meant to score or just put it back into an area, only he will ever know, but the Belgians were back to only a goal behind, and they had 21 minutes of normal time left to make things right.

When the equaliser came five minutes later, it was a body blow to the Japanese. Marouane Fellaini, who had been brought on just before the first goal to cause havoc in the Japanese defence, did just that on 74 minutes when he rose to head the ball home after a great cross from the wing. It made the game 2-2, and with Belgium having the momentum, it felt like it would be hard for Japan to hold them off.

They managed to do it for another 20 minutes, but in the fourth minute of added time, everything fell apart. Japan had valiantly refused to settle for a draw, and the final stages of the match saw both teams pressing for a winner.

But in the 94th minute, a swift Belgian counterattack left Japan flailing. Courtois rolled the ball out to Kevin De Bruyne, who galloped forward looking for the perfect pass. He found it in Meunier out wide, and he clipped the ball back across the box where another substitute, Nacer Chadli, strode onto it and slotted it home in the 94th minute, causing jubilant scenes.

Belgium qualified and went on to win their quarterfinal match against Brazil but came unstuck against the other pre-tournament favourite, France. The golden generation of Belgian football is still together today, and they will hope to go one better and reach the final in Qatar 2022!

They Think It's All Over...

The classic matches remembered in this book are only a handful of those that have occurred at the FIFA World Cup. So many had to be excluded, and if we had tried to cram them all in, you'd be holding something around the size of the New Testament in your hands. Unfortunately, we had to make some tough decisions, but we feel that the 20 that have made it are more than deserving of their place.

But clashes such as England against West Germany in 1990 and Gazza's tears as he received the booking that would have kept him out of the final will never be forgotten. The same goes for the Divine Ponytail, Roberto Baggio, sending the deciding penalty into orbit in the final in '94. Of course, there is Diego Maradona carrying Argentina to the trophy against the Germans in 1986 and so many more that probably deserved to make it too.

The best thing about the World Cup is that it will always come around again, but for some of us, looking back over the best matches and moments is just as enjoyable. We hope that the classics we brought back to life for you here go some way in evoking the fantastic emotions that only the World Cup can bring.

... It Is Now!

You have now come to the end of the book, I really hope you have enjoyed it and have learnt lots of awesome facts about the games' greatest competition to impress your mates and family.

As a small independent publisher, positive reviews left on our books go a long way to attracting new readers who share your passion for the game.

If you are able to take a few minutes out of your day to leave a review it would be greatly appreciated!

If you spot any issues you would like to raise, please do **email me before leaving a negative review** with any comments you may have.

I will be more than happy to liaise with you and can offer refunds or updated copies if you are unhappy with your purchase.

theprofessionalfoulpublishing@gmail.com

Printed in Great Britain
by Amazon

10753492R00050